Evergreen Architecture

Overgrown Buildings and Greener Living

gestalten

Table of Contents

Planting and Planning for an Evergreen Future

The reimagination of our homes, workplaces, and cities—one lushly planted building at a time.

L   egend has it that the Hanging Gardens of Babylon ascended high above an ancient city. Texts describe a magnificent, tiered structure resembling a forested mountain: built from stone, brick, and wood, it held fruit trees and flowering plants that grew in cascades down the multilevel exterior. Today, a rising number of buildings draw upon this fabled example. Green roofs, indoor courtyards, vertical gardens and living facades are increasingly common features in our built landscape. While residents fill the interiors of homes and offices with houseplants, architects are transforming exteriors—reimagining cities as vertical forests, populated by high-rise buildings covered in trees.

Contemporary green architecture—defined here as design that incorporates living, green elements—has emerged in response to environmental issues, caused by sprawling metropolises and the exponential growth of urban populations. By claiming buildings and their component parts as biodiverse natural spaces, the approach explores solutions in the problem itself: decreasing carbon emissions, increasing air quality, and providing habitats for insects and animals—all while addressing the mental and physical health concerns endemic in these contexts.

Today, over half of the global population resides in such urban areas; a figure the United Nations predicts will rise to 68 % by 2050. The UN reports that while cities cover just 3 % of the world's total land area, they account for 60–80 % of the world's energy consumption, over 60 % of resource use, and roughly 70 % of CO_2 emissions globally—a large proportion of which can be linked to buildings. To counteract the considerable burden that our expanding cities place on the planet, architects are turning to green innovation and sustainable practices.

"Architecture has to be instrumental in the fight against climate change," states Koichi Takada, a leading Australia-based architect and vocal advocate for green design in cities. "Buildings are responsible for around 40 % of greenhouse gas emissions in the world. As a first step, we need to stop negatively impacting the environment and depleting the planet's resources. Secondly, we must look at ways of reversing the picture."

To future-proof our cities, we have to slow urban sprawl while simultaneously increasing green cover—architecturally "reversing the picture," to use Takada's phrase. This can only be achieved if we accept our role in the destruction of the natural world and start working to fix it.

Trees and plants are vital to a healthy planet. They release oxygen while removing CO_2 from the air, helping to combat global heating and cooling.

Studies indicate that expanding tree cover in metropolitan centers could help reduce temperatures by almost 5°, in part through their canopies filtering sunshine and providing streets with shade. Nature in cities has also been scientifically proven to make us healthier and happier. Despite this, development continues to prioritize the construction of buildings over the cultivation of green spaces. The green architecture movement consciously counters this, reintroducing nature to cities often in unexpected ways.

Heightened competition for land in urban settlements has seen the popularity of green roofs and rooftop gardens skyrocket. By repurposing spaces that would otherwise go unused, they offer unique, biodiverse oases to plants and insects—as well as their human counterparts. A sustainable innovation, these habitats filter rainfall pollutants, contribute to effective water management systems, and enhance the energy efficiency of the buildings they adorn.

Additionally, such spaces can help mitigate the urban heat island effect: a phenomenon in which a metropolitan center is notably warmer than the rural areas surrounding it, caused by changes to land surface and other human activities. While one green roof lowers the heat of its building, a concentrated number of biodiverse green rooftops would significantly impact that of a city—helping to stymie rising temperatures.

Bill Browning, co-founder of Terrapin Bright Green—a New York-based architecture firm specializing in spaces that incorporate natural elements—describes that people in urban environments are intuitively drawn to green design because it reconnects them with the sights, smells, and textures of nature. This deep-rooted attraction is one of the reasons that houseplants, courtyards, and internal gardens have become such popular features in contemporary architectural design.

In addition to reinforcing this intrinsic link, houseplants serve several purposes. Today, they're as coveted as items of mid-century furniture—and with good reason. Not only do they add vibrancy to interiors, but when introduced at scale, a 1980s NASA study observed that they absorb volatile organic compounds from the air, making them a helpful and attractive houseguest.

Green exteriors are also on the rise. An increasing number of architects are taking plant cover to new heights, designing buildings with green facades, green walls, and vertical gardens. Whether reaching skywards or flowing towards the ground, these lush elements change with the seasons and grow over time, giving architectural spaces an expressive front.

In 2019, Austria-based architecture studio Precht released a hypothetical project, uniting vertical gardening and urban living at an unprecedented scale. As a prototype for modular housing and sustainable agriculture, the Farmhouse addresses two major problems facing cities of the future: population density and access to food. Its towering structure is composed of prefabricated A-frame modules, made from carbon sequestering cross-laminated timber (CLT). The modular nature of the design offers flexible floor plans for both homes and gardens, as well as much-needed high-density housing within a small footprint.

As co-founder Chris Precht explains, the proposal aims to restore an experience far removed from city life, gravitating around self-sufficient, local food production. While focusing on providing sustainable farming systems, the Farmhouse also serves to reduce food miles. "More food will be consumed in the next 50 years than in the last 10,000 years combined, and 80% of it will be consumed in cities," Precht elaborates. "If the majority of people live in urban areas, and if food should be consumed close to where it grows, cities need to become part of a food production loop."

Where others see crisis looming, Precht sees potential for change. "There will be an incentive for architects, city planners, and horticulturalists to create buildings that are more than just expensive real estate," he says. As Precht sees it, urban buildings need to be "more than structures that are isolated from their surroundings—but instead, buildings that are productive members of a neighborhood ecosystem." Green buildings of all sizes will be required to realize this vision, and green design principles are already being applied to projects around the world: from huge, multipurpose developments to single-family dwellings.

←   PLANTERS SURROUND A SEATING AREA IN STUDIO RICK JOY'S TENNYSON 205 IN MEXICO CITY.

The benefits of green architecture extend beyond the tangible production of food and reduction of carbon dioxide: studies show that the introduction of biophilic design imbues spaces with a curative power.

Formzero's Planter Box House in Kuala Lumpur delves into similar ideas, albeit at a much smaller scale. The facade of the three-story tropical home is covered in large concrete boxes, filled with over 40 edible plant varieties. Designed for a retired couple in one of the fastest-growing metropolitan regions in Southeast Asia, Planter Box House is an ode to sustainable and self-sufficient living. The structure incorporates passive design strategies to lower its energy consumption, and each planter collects stormwater, subsequently used to irrigate the tiered green exterior. Like Precht's forward-thinking Farmhouse, this project demonstrates yet again how urban architecture can unite us with—rather than remove us from—nature and agriculture.

The benefits of green architecture extend beyond the tangible production of food and reduction of carbon dioxide: studies show that the introduction of biophilic design imbues spaces with a curative power. Despite the term coming to prominence as recently as the 1980s, biophilia is an enduring concept, shaping the way we have constructed our homes throughout history. The approach heightens our human connection to the environment through the use of natural elements.

Heatherwick Studio's design for Maggie's Leeds—a cancer support center in the United Kingdom—embraces a range of biophilic features for this exact therapeutic reason. Maggie's Centers are open to cancer patients and their support networks, and are designed to provide sanctuary, practical help, and space for recuperation. In Leeds, the studio created a structure resembling an arrangement of rounded planter boxes. Realized using materials such as wood and lime plaster, the end result is a breezy building, populated by plants and flooded with light. Its organic curves mimic forms found in nature, proven to be calming to the eyes and mind. With its heavily planted exterior, the organic building stands in stark contrast to its more sterile and angular surroundings, on the campus of St. James's University Hospital.

→   CHRIS PRECHT'S VISION FOR AN URBAN HIGH-RISE WHERE RESIDENTS GROW THEIR OWN FOOD.

↓   MAGGIE'S LEEDS, A CANCER SUPPORT CENTER DESIGNED USING BIOPHILIC PRINCIPLES AND NO SHORTAGE OF PLANTS, BY THOMAS HEATHERWICK.

groundbreaking Bosco Verticale in Milan. The project is a prototype for a series of towers, which Boeri describes as being "a new format of architectural biodiversity."

This first edition of Bosco Verticale consists of two towers: together housing 800 trees, 15,000 perennials and ground-covering plants, and 5,000 shrubs. Its "complex urban ecosystem" is equivalent to 322,900 square feet (30,000 square meters) of forest, condensed into a 32,000-square-foot (3,000-square-meter) footprint. Tended to by climbing arborists—nicknamed the "Flying Gardeners"—and watered using an advanced irrigation system, it is a spectacularly verdant anomaly that enriches Milan's skyline.

During the design phase of the project, the studio worked with a team of specialist engineers, botanists, and agronomists to devise a structure that could bear the weight, growth, and movement of so many trees—a challenge, given that there was no literature on the subject. To prevent potential wind damage, larger specimens are planted in steel cages embedded into reinforced concrete planters. Each planter is connected to the terrace above using a steel cable, as well as being linked to the tree by elastic belts: limiting potential movement without hindering the plant's growth.

Boeri first imagined a tower covered in trees, rather than reflective cladding, during a 2007 visit to Dubai. Tracing his arboreal obsession back to reading Italo Calvino's 1957 novel *The Baron in the Trees*—in which a boy abandons the ground to spend his life among the branches—Bosco Verticale offers a similar escape. Alongside other large-scale projects that incorporate greenery, it offers a vision of cities of the future: vertical streets, vertical forests, and a different kind of nature.

On the other side of the world, Koichi Takada has embarked on a mission of similar heights: demonstrating green architecture's potential to solve climate problems with the soon-to-be constructed Urban Forest. This carbon-neutral high-rise will host over 1,000 trees and 20,000 plants, sourced from 259 native Australian species, and once completed, will be the country's greenest building. Takada describes the project as the "evolution of mass greening," because of the holistic way it considers sustainability.

The high-rise isn't green simply because it's covered in plants, but because every element of its design and construction has been weighed from an environmental perspective. "Urban Forest's goal is to naturalize and humanize architecture," says Takada. "The project's impact extends far beyond the physical boundaries of the site. It includes a new farm outside the city that serves as a source for the trees that will be integrated into the building."

The 30-story building and its accompanying tree farm will be located in Brisbane, the capital of Queensland—known as Australia's Sunshine State. The farm will continue growing trees beyond those needed for the building, as a means of offsetting the tower's emissions during operation. "Our future cities need to include regenerative architecture and be carbon positive, balancing any emissions from the existing building stock," believes Takada. "They need to play a central role in the reforestation of our planet, restoring its resources and positively impacting the well-being of its inhabitants."

This approach recognizes that the need for sustainable green architecture has never been more pertinent. "The predominant paradigms governing architecture at any given time usually stem from the need to address the most pressing challenges of the day," he explains. "Today, we are facing the problems that we created ourselves over the last two centuries. The Industrial Revolution, followed by both world wars, were the destruction not just of our cities, cultures, and population, but of our nature too. Bringing back nature and restoring it is imperative."

At surface level, green architecture offers us an aesthetic reprieve from the concrete continuity of the built environment, providing a connection to nature, and imbuing spaces with its healing benefits. If you look deeper, it has the capacity to reimagine our cities and our lives, in ways that are both sustainable and beautiful. This book explores recent examples of a movement that is now well underway. It also provides glimpses of possible futures where—as people once wrote of ancient Babylon—towers resembling tree-covered mountains populate the skyline.

With a flourishing rooftop garden, full of native English species and inspired by the local Yorkshire woodlands, the center is also surrounded by areas of evergreens, providing continuous color over the winter months. Visitors and patients alike are encouraged to tend to the 17,000 plants and 23,000 bulbs around the site, expanding on a crucial element of biophilia—touch. As founder Thomas Heatherwick explains, "By only using natural, sustainable materials and immersing the building in thousands of plants, there was a chance for us to make an extraordinary environment capable of inspiring visitors with hope and perseverance during their difficult health journeys."

But no movement is without its problems. When greenery is applied as a hasty afterthought, or considered simply an aesthetic trend, it is often counterproductive to environmental goals. Without the input of specialized landscape architects, botanists, or horticulturalists, planting can be implemented using the wrong infrastructure and with minimal consideration given to setting, light, and the appropriateness of chosen varieties. This becomes costly—draining energy, labor, and water, and giving little in return.

To design sustainable green spaces, architects must move beyond aesthetics to consider the financial, practical, and environmental implications of their endeavors: Will the building be strong enough to bear the weight of the plants? How much additional infrastructure does this require? How does a green wall actually contribute to its surroundings? Where do the species come from, and what care do they need? Will they survive if they aren't native? Is the design environmentally friendly, or does it just look "green"?

Italian architect Stefano Boeri is used to such questions. Together with a team of experts, in 2014 Stefano Boeri Architetti completed the

↑   LUCIANO PIA'S 25 VERDE, WHICH INTEGRATES MORE THAN 100 TREES ALONG ITS FACADE.
←   THOMAS HEATHERWICK'S 20-STORY RESIDENTIAL SKYSCRAPER IN SINGAPORE,
    WHERE EACH TERRACE IS A GARDEN.

Mill Valley Cabins

Feldman Architecture

MILL VALLEY, CA, USA

↑   THE LOWER CABIN'S ROOFTOP GARDEN IS PLANTED IN EYE-CATCHING, UNDULATING
     STRIPES.
→   PERCHED ON A HILL, THE CABINS OVERLOOK THE IMPRESSIVE FOREST OF MILL VALLEY.

The magnificent pines and redwoods of Mill Valley were a long-standing fixture for this project's clients, already living on site. It was essential that the pair of additional cabins—containing an art studio and a yoga space—celebrate this natural beauty by nestling into their green surroundings. Feldman Architecture designed structures that perch lightly on the sloping woodland, leaving tree roots undisturbed, while landscaping and natural materials help the buildings blend into the forest. The roof of the lower cabin is a cultivated garden, creating a lush view from the art studio. This garden is also integral to the site's stormwater management, collecting and distributing rainwater in a controlled way to prevent ground erosion. The cabin exteriors are clad in subtly weathered wood, while their windows and skylights frame ethereal views. The resulting spaces serve to enhance the beauty of the forest, providing intimate places of creativity and calm.

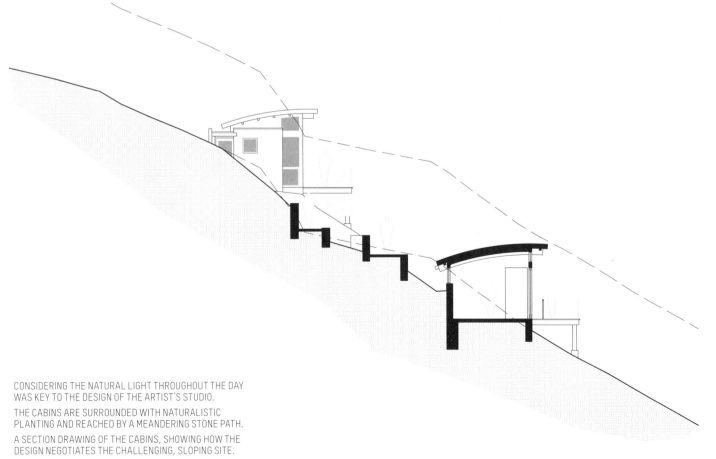

↑   CONSIDERING THE NATURAL LIGHT THROUGHOUT THE DAY
    WAS KEY TO THE DESIGN OF THE ARTIST'S STUDIO.

→   THE CABINS ARE SURROUNDED WITH NATURALISTIC
    PLANTING AND REACHED BY A MEANDERING STONE PATH.

↗   A SECTION DRAWING OF THE CABINS, SHOWING HOW THE
    DESIGN NEGOTIATES THE CHALLENGING, SLOPING SITE.

Atelier Villa

Formafatal

PLAYA HERMOSA, COSTA RICA

Merging with its wild surroundings, the elegant form of Atelier Villa floats just above the jungle floor. This 85-foot-long (26-meter-long) residence looks out onto breathtaking panoramic views of green hills and distant ocean. Nestled into a slope, three sides of the slender structure are fitted with perforated, rust-colored aluminum panels, inviting the ocean breeze within. Doubling as canopies when raised, a specialized coating prevents the heating and corrosion of the metal. Meanwhile, the rear facade is clad in black, charred wood, treated using a traditional Japanese technique that preserves and waterproofs the timber. Deliberately left windowless, this creates privacy for utility, bathroom, and kitchen areas in the design. An expansive green roof allows the building's profile to all but disappear into the hillside, as well as providing the thermal mass to keep it cool. Furniture made by local craftspeople completes a home that celebrates its unique tropical location.

↑ THE LUXURIOUS VILLA SITS WITHIN THE DENSE COSTA RICAN JUNGLE, OVERLOOKING THE COASTLINE.

An expansive green roof allows the
building's profile to all but disappear
into the hillside, as well as providing
the thermal mass to keep it cool.

↑   THE VILLA OPENS OUT TO THE SURROUNDING VERDANT LANDSCAPES.

→   THE FLOORPLAN SHOWS THE TERRACES WRAPPING AROUND THE LIVING SPACE.

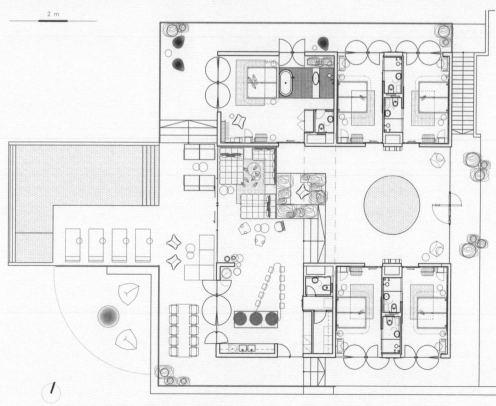

2 m

Treetop Hotel Løvtag

Sigurd Larsen

MARIAGER FJORD, DENMARK

This simple reinvention of the tree house is the perfect woodland retreat and together, three of Sigurd Larsen's structures form Denmark's first treetop hotel. By wrapping a wooden cabin around the trunk of a living tree, each playful hideaway allows for a multisensory experience of the forest. Visitors are able to touch, smell, and live alongside the central tree, while enjoying expansive views of their forest surroundings. The cabin is accessed using a suspended wooden bridge, strung in a gentle ramp from the mossy ground below. Its minimalist interior is simply lined in warm-toned wood, creating a peaceful and cozy haven. A shower area, clad in perforated metal screens, cantilevers off the structure and provides the unique opportunity to bathe among trees and dappled sunlight. Ascending a small wooden staircase, guests gain magical rooftop views—and the feeling they could keep climbing to the very top of the canopy.

↑   SET WITHIN A DENSE DANISH FOREST, EACH CABIN IS RAISED ON HIGH STILTS AND WRAPS AROUND A TREE TRUNK.

↑   INSIDE THE CABIN'S COZY, TIMBER-CLAD INTERIOR, GENEROUS WINDOWS FRAME FOREST VIEWS.

←   THE ROOF TERRACE OFFERS GUESTS THE CHANCE TO ENJOY 360-DEGREE WOODLAND VIEWS.

→   THE BARE TRUNK RUNS THROUGH THE CENTER OF THE LIVING SPACE, EMULATING A TREE HOUSE.

Landaburu Borda

Jordi Hidalgo Tané Arquitectura

BERA, NAVARRE, SPAIN

In rural Navarre in northern Spain, Jordi Hidalgo Tané has added a buried annex, molded by the mountainous landscape, to a traditional stone building. Preserving the original character of the tall farmhouse, the extension is hidden within the adjacent hillside and accessed via a nearly invisible glass corridor. This new wing of the house contains an open-plan living, kitchen, and dining area and features a dynamic concrete roof, set into the contours of the ground above. Cleverly placed skylights create the illusion of a cantilevered roof, and a wall of glass spanning the length of the structure frames panoramic views of its surroundings. Inside the farmhouse, the introduction of a minimal steel and wood staircase and shuttered concrete walls echo the palette of materials in the annex. The connecting glass corridor is dotted with plants, blurring the distinction between indoors and outdoors. By anchoring these new additions to the existing structure and the site, Hidalgo Tané has created unique and exciting spaces that honor their mountain location.

→   THE GLASS CORRIDOR CONNECTING THE REFURBISHED FARMHOUSE
    AND THE NEW, RECESSED EXTENSION.

← THE ANNEX IS EMBEDDED INTO A GRASSY HILL AND TOPPED BY A GREEN ROOF, MINIMIZING ITS IMPACT ON THE NATURAL BEAUTY OF THE SITE.

↘ THE TRADITIONAL FARMHOUSE AND ADJACENT CONCRETE EXTENSION, JOINED BY A GLASS CORRIDOR.

↓ WITH GLASS WALLS ON THREE SIDES, THE EXTENSION'S OPEN-PLAN LIVING SPACE ALSO FEATURES A DYNAMIC CONCRETE ROOF.

→   SKYLIGHTS SEPARATING THE HEAVY CONCRETE ROOF FROM THE VOLUME OF THE LANDSCAPE GIVE THE IMPRESSION IT
     COULD BE FLOATING.
↓   THE ANNEX'S OVERHANGING AWNING AND CONSTANT GROUND LEVEL MERGE THE LIVING AREA AND THE OUTDOORS.

Writer's Shed

Matt Gibson Architecture + Design

MELBOURNE, AUSTRALIA

There is an innate feeling of sanctuary to this cozy, camouflaged retreat. A simple box cloaked in dark-green ivy, the intimate outbuilding was designed to create a calm space for writing and reflection within the client's garden. Beneath this vegetation, the structure is coated in a waterproof rubber membrane which protects and insulates it from the elements. Its interior walls, ceiling, and floor are clad in warm-toned, sustainable, hoop pine plywood. Boston ivy was chosen for being evergreen, fast-growing, and easy to maintain—providing the uninterrupted natural cover the concept required. The modest single space has two entrances—one to the garden, the other to the lane behind—allowing it to receive deliveries and guests. A skylight brings natural light into the heart of the interior, while a simple fixed window sits above a desk, framing the garden beyond. Rather than obstructing views from the house, this project is a characterful addition that enhances its surrounding natural landscape.

↑ A LARGE, FIXED WINDOW PERFECTLY FRAMES THE WRITER AT THEIR DESK, SURROUNDED BY IVY.

← PLYWOOD PANELING COVERS THE INTERIOR, CREATING A COZY AND NATURAL FEELING.

← FAST-GROWING BOSTON IVY CREATES
A DENSE COAT OF GREENERY THAT
COMPLETELY COVERS THE SHED'S
WATERPROOF MEMBRANE.

↑ POSITIONED OPPOSITE THE GLASS
DOOR LEADING TO THE GARDEN, A
SECOND, MIRROR-COVERED DOOR
GRANTS ACCESS TO THE LANE BEHIND.

→ THE SIMPLY DECORATED INTERIOR,
WITH STORAGE FOR BOOKS AND
TOOLS, PROVIDES A BLANK CANVAS
FOR CREATIVITY.

Blooming Bamboo Home

H&P Architects

HANOI, VIETNAM

In response to the displacement of people and damage to homes caused by severe weather in Vietnam, H&P Architects created this prototype for an adaptable modular house. Built almost entirely from renewable, natural materials—such as fast-growing, affordable, and abundant bamboo, coconut leaves, and fiberboard—the structure can be assembled by inhabitants in only 25 days. Its modular character allows it to be expanded to suit the needs of the site and its users, whether functioning as a home, school, or medical center. The building is elevated on stilts, providing storage space for food or livestock below and preparing it to withstand floodwaters of up to 5 feet (1.5 meters). Walls and segments of the roof can be opened up, ventilating the space and allowing natural light to enter. Although the design is deeply functional, the architects' intelligent use of materials and understanding of atmosphere have also created a space of simple beauty.

→ RAISED ON STILTS, THIS FLOOD-RESISTANT PROTOTYPE IS PREDOMINANTLY BUILT USING RENEWABLE MATERIALS.

← PARTS OF THE STRUCTURE CAN BE
  FOLDED BACK AND PROPPED OPENED,
  ADJUSTING LIGHT AND SHADE AND
  CREATING OPEN-AIR PLATFORMS.

↑ VARIATION IN THE DIRECTION AND
  DENSITY OF THE BAMBOO PANELS
  ACHIEVES A BEAUTIFUL, SCREENED
  QUALITY OF LIGHT.

→ THICKER SECTIONS OF BAMBOO ARE
  USED AS HANGING PLANTERS IN A
  LIGHTWEIGHT VERTICAL GARDEN.

Meier Road

Mork-Ulnes Architects

SEBASTOPOL, CA, USA

In a building complex housing an artist's studio and home, Mork-Ulnes Architects have created functional spaces full of personality. Built on the site of a run-down barn, the main structure contains a studio, office, and living and storage areas. The introduction of an inverted pitched roof—a playful twist on the original—maximizes the bright light needed in the client's workspace. Sustainable, recycled cladding paints bold stripes of weathered timber on the facade, introducing eye-catching texture to the site while honoring its agricultural past. The architects deliver an entirely different mood in the adjoining building, nicknamed the Amoeba. Its organic form seems to grow from the side of the angular barn, with lush plantings set in island-like patches in the smooth concrete floor. Greenery is slowly transforming this section of the home into a jungle—one in which to cook, eat, and entertain.

↑ THE BRIGHT, PLANT-FILLED INTERIOR OF THE AMOEBA—ONE OF TWO BUILDINGS ON THE SITE.

→   ISLANDS OF PLANTING ARE SET INTO THE AMOEBA'S CONCRETE FLOOR, ALLOWING NATURE TO THRIVE ALONGSIDE
      THE INHABITANTS OF THE HOME.
↓   THE LIGHTWEIGHT STEEL STAIRCASE OF THE TIMBER-CLAD BARN, WHICH CONTAINS THE STUDIO AND LIVING SPACES.

Sloped Villa

Studio Okami Architecten

MONT-DE-L'ENCLUS, HAINAUT, BELGIUM

Studio Okami Architecten's sensitive addition to this Belgian valley melds with the hillside, hidden behind an elegant brick colonnade. A single-story structure topped with a green roof, the building was conceived to all but disappear into the landscape, while creating a generous home that celebrates its beautiful outlook. Its incognito profile was key to gaining local authorities' approval—in an area in which regulations stipulate pitched roofs, local brick, and predefined window sizes. In this non-traditional design, the entire front portion of the rectangular home benefits from floor-to-ceiling windows, offering unobstructed views of the valley beyond. Two brick staircases at either side of the house lead up to the roof garden and surrounding hillside, while a glassed-in courtyard brings natural light into the heart of the home. Cozy, cave-like bedrooms are buried deeper into the slope, toward the rear of the layout. Sheltered by the earth, an interior palette of muted materials draws the eye to the stunning greenery outdoors.

→　THE HOUSE'S SIMPLE BRICK COLONNADE EMERGES FROM THE GRASSY SLOPE.

↑   A CENTRAL COURTYARD CREATES A
    PRIVATE INDOOR GARDEN, AS WELL AS
    DRAWING NATURAL LIGHT DEEP INTO
    THE HOME.

↗   A FREESTANDING BATH SITS NEXT TO
    THE COURTYARD—PROVIDING GREEN
    VIEWS WHILE BATHING.

→   THE BUILDING'S SIMPLE COMBINATION
    OF BRICK, SHUTTERED CONCRETE, AND
    MUTED WOOD ACCENTS RETAIN FOCUS
    ON THE LANDSCAPE BEYOND.

← MASKED BY THE COLONNADE, BRICK STEPS ON EITHER SIDE OF THE HOME ALLOW FOR ACCESS TO THE ROOF GARDEN AND SURROUNDING HILLSIDE.

↘ THE GREEN ROOF EFFECTIVELY CAMOUFLAGES THE BUILDING—VIEWED HERE FROM ABOVE.

↓ BY BURYING THE REAR OF THE HOUSE IN THE SLOPE, THE IMPACT OF ITS PROFILE IS MINIMIZED.

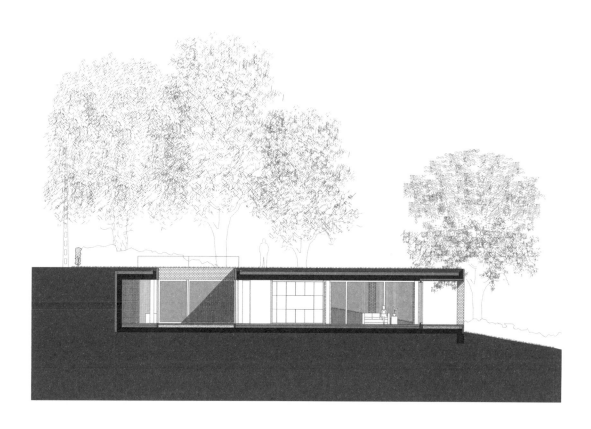

Sun Path House

Studio Christian Wassmann

MIAMI BEACH, FL, USA

Sun Path House was designed, first and foremost, as a place for the well-being of a renowned chef and his family. Commissioned as an extension to their single-story 1930s home, architect Christian Wassmann's design provides sheltered outdoor spaces for cooking and entertaining, with a self-contained master bedroom and private rooftop above. A floating green box punctured by a spiraling wall, the building's central concrete structure forms the main staircase—and doubles as a chimney for an outdoor pizza oven. Rough and rugged concrete forms are enveloped by climbing green vines, framing every view and acting as a veil against the hot Florida sun. As its name suggests, the sculptural spiral also maps the path of the sun during the summer solstice, inspired by the precise geometries of India's ancient Jantar Mantar observatory. The rooftop is intended as a secluded solarium—a contemplative space, sheltered from the wind and open to the sky.

↑   THE UNIQUE EXTENSION IS WRAPPED WITH A LIGHTWEIGHT WIRE TRELLIS, SUPPORTING THE GROWTH OF GREEN VINES.

↗   THE VINES ACT AS A SCREEN,
     SHADING THE WINDOWS FROM
     THE FLORIDA SUNSHINE.

→   THE CENTRAL CONCRETE SPIRAL DERIVES
     ITS FORM FROM THE PATH OF THE SUN
     DURING THE SUMMER SOLSTICE.

↓   THE GREENERY ALSO CREATES PRIVACY,
     ACHIEVING AN INTIMATE BUT OPEN
     FEELING TO THE LIVING QUARTERS.

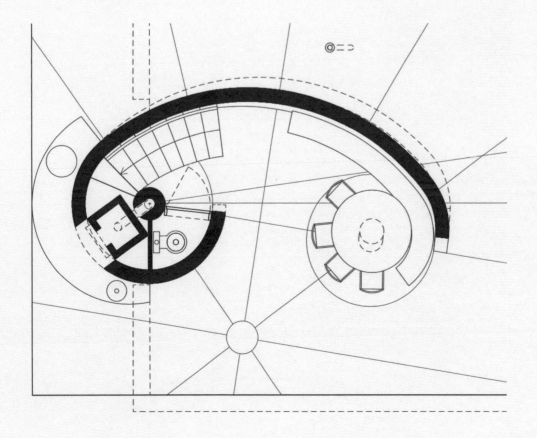

← THE GREEN VINES SOFTEN THE
 EXTENSION'S UPPER VOLUME, WHICH
 MIGHT OTHERWISE DWARF THE EXISTING
 ADJACENT BUNGALOW.

↑ THE SCULPTURAL SPIRAL STAIRCASE
 PROVIDES THE PERFECT SHELTERED
 SPACE IN WHICH TO ENJOY THE SKY.

↗ THE GROUND FLOOR PLAN, ILLUSTRATING
 THE ASTRONOMICAL GEOMETRY OF THE
 CONCRETE WALL.

Sun Rain Rooms

Tonkin Liu

LONDON, U. K.

Though London's climate has a reputation for being rainy and gray, this unique and futuristic addition to a Georgian town house celebrates nature and the local weather. Envisioned as a multilayered urban garden, the project was designed as an extension to the home and studio of Tonkin Liu founders Anna Liu and Mike Tonkin. The focal point of the scheme is an organically curved and glass-paneled space, wrapped around a patio—which, at the press of a button, can be transformed into a shallow reflecting pool, filled with rainwater collected on top of the main building. From beneath the structure's arched canopy, occupants can watch for ripples in the water and reflections of the sky above. On top of the canopy sits a verdant roof garden studded with droplet-like glass oculi that allow shafts of natural light to enter the interior below. A basement level contains a bedroom and bathrooms, with a plant-filled light well introducing greenery to the most intimate quarters of the home. Within a compact site, Tonkin Liu has achieved an otherworldly space in which to appreciate a rainy city.

→   THE VIEW FROM BENEATH THE CURVED OUTDOOR CANOPY, LOOKING TOWARD THE REFLECTING POOL AND MAIN BUILDING.

↑   PASSERSBY WOULD NEVER SUSPECT THAT A FUTURISTIC ADDITION IS HIDING BEHIND THIS ELEGANT GEORGIAN TOWN HOUSE.

→   THE EXTENSION'S CURVED FORM IS COVERED BY A RESILIENT GREEN ROOF, SCATTERED WITH GLASS OCULI.

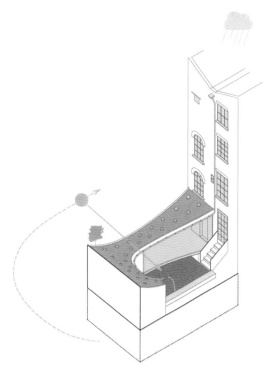

↖ THE FORM OF THE EXTENSION FOLLOWS
   THE PATH OF THE SUN THROUGHOUT THE
   DAY, MAXIMIZING SUNSHINE IN THE
   NARROW SPACE.

← TOWARDS THE REAR OF THE OPEN-AIR
   PATIO IS A SHELTERED DINING SPACE,
   SEPARATED FROM STORAGE, WORK, AND
   COOKING AREAS BY A MIRRORED WALL.

↓ RAINDROPS FALL INTO THE REFLECTING
   POOL—THEIR RIPPLES CAN BE ENJOYED
   FROM INDOORS.

↑   A LIGHT WELL, POSITIONED NEAR THE
     EXISTING HOUSE, DRAWS NATURAL
     LIGHT INTO THE BEDROOM BELOW.

↗   A CURVED PARTITION OF WARM-TONED
     WOOD WRAPS AROUND THE ROOM,
     CREATING A COZY ATMOSPHERE—AND
     A HEADBOARD FOR THE BED.

→   THE EXTENSION IS FILLED WITH
     PLANTS, TRANSFORMING THE INTERIOR
     INTO AN ALTERNATIVE GARDEN.

Daita2019

Built as a home for a multigenerational family, daita2019 proposes an urban lifestyle still intertwined with nature. Despite the compact site, Yamada has designed spaces that flow between the indoors and outdoors, integrating the garden into the residents' everyday lives. Readily available and affordable metal scaffolding is used to create a structure for plants and trees that can easily be reconfigured. Terraces are carefully placed to provide platforms for harvesting fruit and other produce, as well as offering outdoor spaces that can be enjoyed from the upper levels of the house. In summer, doors and windows open to allow fresh, cool air from the garden to flow into the building; in winter, low sun shining through the structure's glass facade passively warms the home. Inside, the main timber structure is left largely exposed, with wooden beams acting as informal divisions of space—as if living in a forest among the trees. Yamada strikes an intriguing balance between static, man-made elements and the seasonal changes of the garden as it continues to grow.

Suzuko Yamada Architects

TOKYO, JAPAN

↑   THE SCAFFOLDING WEAVES THROUGH
     THE GREENERY, CREATING PLATFORMS
     THAT CAN BE ADAPTED IN THE FUTURE.

↗   INSIDE THE HOME, YAMADA HAS
     MINIMIZED THE USE OF PARTITION
     WALLS, WITH TIMBER STRUCTURES
     SEPARATING SPACES LIKE BRANCHES.

→   PLATFORMS ARE DESIGNED TO WRAP
     AROUND TREES, ALLOWING FOR
     THE HARVESTING OF FRUIT AND
     RESIDENTS' CLOSE-UP ENJOYMENT
     OF BLOSSOMING PLANTS.

House in Tsukimiyama

Tato Architects

TSUKIMIYAMA, JAPAN

An unassuming corrugated steel exterior might give the impression of a humble industrial building, but inside is an urban sanctuary and family home. At the heart of the structure, a simple pitched roof features large skylights on the eastern side, flooding an inner courtyard and garden with natural light. The glass panels overhead were intended to all but disappear, making the interior feel open to the elements. Despite the huge expanses of glass, carefully designed ventilation brings fresh air into the home, keeping it comfortable throughout the year. The courtyard provides living space among its planting and features a bathroom annex in the corner, separated by a simple curtain. In a playful addition, the toilet is housed in a closet—creating privacy while being a humorous take on old-fashioned outhouses. A lightweight wooden bridge runs above the garden area, connecting rooms on the upper floor. The design successfully reimagines the garden as a space inside the home, allowing it to be inhabited and enjoyed every day.

↑   THE SHELTERED GARDEN AT THE HEART OF THE HOME, SPANNED BY A WOODEN BRIDGE CONNECTING ROOMS ON THE UPPER FLOOR.

←   THE VIEW OF THE HOUSE FROM THE STREET, WITH ITS UNASSUMING CORRUGATED METAL CLADDING.

↑   THE MAIN LIVING SPACES WERE DESIGNED TO MELD WITH THE GARDEN, ENCOURAGING A DAILY CONNECTION TO NATURE.

←   THE UPSTAIRS ROOMS BENEFIT FROM THE ABUNDANT NATURAL LIGHT CHANNELED INTO THE CENTRAL GARDEN SPACE.

→   DESIGNED WITH THE FAMILY IN MIND, THE GARDEN PROVIDES EDIBLE PRODUCE AND A SHELTERED SPACE TO PLAY IN THROUGHOUT THE YEAR.

↑ THE SNAKING FORM OF THIS HABITAT HORTICULTURE INSTALLATION EXPLORES THE POSSIBILITIES OF URBAN SURFACES.

→ THE CORNER'S COLORFUL PLANTING STANDS OUT IN ITS DOWNTOWN SURROUNDINGS.

Cedar Alley

Habitat Horticulture

SAN FRANCISCO, CA, USA

This small-scale project by Habitat Horticulture exhibits the potential for adding greenery and nature through limited city spaces. Straddling a corner in San Francisco's gritty Tenderloin neighborhood, the installation was designed to resemble a living creature climbing the walls. Its geometric form snakes up the building in two bright streaks of plantings, softening the block's dark-gray facade. The designers carefully selected resilient plant varieties, supported by an integrated maintenance system—maximizing the installation's longevity and impact. Rather than providing a backdrop, this landscaping is an eye-catching focal point in the local area, and holds its own against the man-made environment. Too often we walk around cities with our eyes fixed forward, or down at our devices. This small intervention encourages us to look up and engage with the natural world, even in the most urban of settings.

Garden-house

MAD Architects

BEVERLY HILLS, CA, USA

Gardenhouse is a playful contribution to this Beverly Hills neighborhood, combining the architectural language of an urban apartment block with that of a hillside village. In MAD Architects' first project in the United States, the Chinese studio wanted to respond to its ordered and carefully maintained Los Angeles setting. The site's ground floor shops are crowned with a living green wall planted in painterly swaths of color and containing a variety of residential units. The white, pitched roofs of these homes grow out above this verdant green band, adding a refreshing domesticity to the urban surroundings. The architects created light, airy spaces within this rooftop village, while the lower level features curving, gray walls that lend an organic, cave-like feeling. A landscaped courtyard and reflecting pool offer communal space for refuge and contemplation, and all of this only a stone's throw from the city's bustling boulevards.

→   GARDENHOUSE AS SEEN FROM THE STREET, WITH ITS DISTINCT BAND
    OF GREENERY TOPPED BY A CLUSTER OF PITCHED ROOFS.

← THE WHITE PITCHED ROOF RESIDENCES CREATE THE FEELING OF A VILLAGE ON TOP OF THIS URBAN SITE.

↖ LOWER RESIDENTIAL UNITS ARE WRAPPED IN A LIVING GREEN WALL, SOFTENING THE BUILDING'S FACADE.

↓ THE LOWER LEVELS' USE OF FORM AND MATERIALS CREATE SHELTERED, COOL SPACES.

← THE TEXTURED GREENERY
OF THE FACADE CONTRASTS
WITH BRIGHT, WHITE, CLEAN
INTERIOR SPACES.

→ THE DIVISION OF THE EXTERIOR
INTO THREE DISTINCT BANDS
GIVES A MORE HUMAN SCALE
TO THE BUILDING.

↓ THE GREEN WALL IS PLANTED TO
CREATE A DYNAMIC PATTERN OF
DIFFERING COLORS AND TEXTURES.

Biesbosch Museum Island

Studio Marco Vermeulen

WERKENDAM, NETHERLANDS

Located on a man-made island in the wetlands of the De Biesbosch National Park, Studio Marco Vermeulen has transformed this local museum: adding a 11,000-square-foot (1,000-square-meter) wing, immersive roofscape, and freshwater tidal park. A green roof blankets the scheme, with a weaving walkway that encourages visitors to explore the terrain. The new wing incorporates generous expanses of floor-to-ceiling, heat-resistant windows, looking out onto the marshland surroundings. River water flows through underfloor pipes to effectively cool the building. During colder months, a sustainable biomass stove warms the building using the same system. Sanitary wastewater passes through a willow filter—the first of its kind in the Netherlands—before running back into the wetlands. Willow absorbs elements such as nitrogen and phosphate, nourishing its growth; the wood can later be used as fuel for the biomass stove. This project exemplifies design that integrates sustainable technologies while enhancing the experience of nature—promising new discoveries with every visit.

→   THE MUSEUM BUILDING IS BLANKETED WITH A MOSSY GREEN ROOF, CREATING A
    SURREAL TOPOGRAPHY.

← THE SOARING GLASS ELEVATIONS OF THE NEW MUSEUM WING EMERGE FROM THE SLOPING LANDSCAPE.

↘ THE DESIGN OF THE NEW WING TAKES THE FORM OF ANGULAR HILLS AND VALLEYS.

↓ A RIVER-LIKE INSTALLATION FLOWS THROUGH THE INTERIOR, EDUCATING VISITORS ON BIODIVERSITY AND THE SITE'S TECHNOLOGICAL INNOVATION.

↑   THE MUSEUM IS LOCATED ON AN
     ARTIFICIAL ISLAND, WITHIN A PROTECTED
     WETLAND HABITAT.

↗   THE SITE'S NEW ADDITIONS MAINTAIN
     A LOW PROFILE WHILE PROVIDING
     IMPACTFUL, BRIGHT SPACES—AS SHOWN
     IN THIS ELEVATION.

→   A ROOFTOP WALKWAY CHARTS A
     TRAIL THROUGH THE ROOFSCAPE,
     INVITING EXPLORATION.

Birch Moss Chapel

↑   VIEWED AT A DISTANCE, THE STRUCTURE BLENDS INTO THE SURROUNDING FOREST OF ELEGANT BIRCH TREES.
→   THE GLASS ROOF IS SUPPORTED BY A STEEL STRUCTURE, CONCEALED INSIDE TREE TRUNKS.

Kengo Kuma & Associates

KARUIZAWA, JAPAN

Kengo Kuma is renowned for his pioneering use of structural timber, inspired by traditional Japanese architecture. With this project Kuma takes a radically naturalistic approach, obliterating a building into its wooded surroundings. After opening in 2012, the Karuizawa New Art Museum—located in a resort town approximately 100 miles (161 kilometers) west of Tokyo—became a popular venue for weddings. This led them to commission Kuma to design a chapel that celebrated art and the romantic landscape of the grounds. In response, Kuma collaborated with French artist Jean-Michel Othoniel, who created a number of heart-shaped sculptures for the site. A steel structure hidden within silver birch trunks supports a lightweight glass roof. Transparent pews, and moss that covers the ground indoors and out, dissolve conventional boundaries further still. The result is a sanctuary that venerates nature in its purest form.

The Living Wall at SFMOMA

Habitat Horticulture

SAN FRANCISCO, CA, USA

Habitat Horticulture has created nothing short of a living work of art at the San Francisco Museum of Modern Art. Located within the 2016 expansion of the museum by architects Snøhetta, the two-story, 150-foot-long (46-meter-long) installation introduces an iconic ribbon of green into the tower-dominated neighborhood. Contrasting with the smooth and sculptural, creamy-white facade of the building, the vertical garden creates a beautiful backdrop for sculpture in the adjacent terrace and museum interior, as well as a space of calm. The 16,000 plants on the wall comprised of 38 species planted in carefully composed swaths across its surface, precisely watered and maintained by an advanced sensor and irrigation system. Far from a static piece, the wall is designed to transform seasonally and encourage its own evolving ecosystem. David Brenner, founder of Habitat Horticulture, recommends walking the vast length of the wall as if it were a forest trail, for a multisensory experience.

→   THE LIVING WALL, SEEN HERE FROM INSIDE THE MUSEUM, WAS CAREFULLY
    DESIGNED TO TRANSFORM WITH THE SEASONS.

↑ VISITORS ARE ENCOURAGED TO APPROACH THE WALL AND EXPERIENCE ITS EFFECT CLOSE-UP—UNLIKE SOME OF THE ART!

← ANGULAR SCULPTURE AND THE ORGANIC TEXTURES OF THE GREEN WALL FORM AN INTRIGUING DIALOGUE.

→ GLIMPSED FROM THE MAIN FOYER, THE LIVING WALL DRAWS VISITORS UP INTO THE MUSEUM'S OUTDOOR TERRACE.

Kö-Bogen II

Ingenhoven Architects

DÜSSELDORF, GERMANY

An extraordinary 5 miles (8 kilometers) of hornbeam hedges cover this sustainable project in Düsseldorf. Containing office, retail, and recreation spaces, the green design responds to its urban context. A glass facade looks out onto one of the city's busiest shopping streets, while the site as a whole incorporates a public square and garden. The main building's profile slopes down toward this plaza, mimicking a hillside, and interacting with a smaller triangular structure with an accessible green roof. Hornbeam, an evergreen species native to Germany, was chosen for its combination of maximum greenery and minimal maintenance. The hedges produce new, light-green leaves in spring, darkening to rich green and golden brown later in the year—transforming the exterior with the seasons. Pioneers of sustainable architecture since 1985, Kö-Bogen II reinforces Ingenhoven Architects' position at the forefront of the green building movement.

↑   THE ADJACENT BUILDINGS OF KÖ-BOGEN II, WHICH SLOPE DOWNWARDS TO FORM A VALLEY-LIKE PUBLIC PLAZA.

← BY ANGLING THE SIDE OF THE MAIN VOLUME, THE SCHEME BALANCES OPEN PUBLIC SPACE WITH THE HEIGHT OF ITS ARCHITECTURAL SURROUNDINGS.

↘ THE GREEN FACADE TEMPERS THE SCALE OF THE BUILDING, SUGGESTING AN URBAN HILLSIDE.

↓ THE DESIGN OF THE HEDGES MIXES MATTER WITH ANGULAR FORMS.

Oasis Terraces

Serie Architects and Multiply Architects

SINGAPORE

Redefining the exclusive reputation of roof gardens, Oasis Terraces offers an accessible, public green space. In a city where land comes at a premium, the design layers a park over a combined community, healthcare, and shopping center in the dense Punggol area. Ramps create a multidimensional landscape spanning six stories, climbing from a covered public plaza and adjacent waterfront up to top-floor gardens that form a natural amphitheater. Far from a solely aesthetic choice, the intention is to use these areas for urban farming and community projects. The architects describe how, "by bringing residents together to plant, maintain, and enjoy them, the gardens help nourish community bonds." Part of a new generation of community centers for Singapore's social housing residents, the project sets a new standard in generosity and greenery within the city's public spaces.

→ THE VIEW FROM THE TOP OF THE BUILDING, REACHED VIA A SLOPING TOPOGRAPHY OF RAMPS.

← WALKWAYS NAVIGATE THE FULL HEIGHT OF THE STRUCTURE, ENABLING PUBLIC ACCESS TO THE ROOFTOP GARDENS.
↓ THE WINDOWS ARE SET BACK, CREATING SHADED BALCONIES FILLED WITH PLANTS THAT OFFER ADDITIONAL, INTIMATE GREEN SPACES.

↑ ENCOMPASSING A HUGE SITE, THE DESIGN'S LANDSCAPING AND COVERED PUBLIC PLAZA SERVE TO INTEGRATE THE BLOCK INTO ITS CONTEXT.

→ THE COMBINATION OF MINIMAL WHITE FACADES AND OVERFLOWING GREENERY EMBODIES SINGAPORE'S URBAN AND NATURAL IDENTITIES.

Urban Forest

Koichi Takada Architects

BRISBANE, AUSTRALIA

Not just an iconic addition to the Brisbane skyline, Urban Forest is a statement on the potential for greening cities worldwide. This ambitious experiment in reconnecting urban environments with nature—for completion in 2024—turns our expectation of high-rise city living on its head. The 30-story tower will house nearly 400 apartments, with a shared rooftop garden and a public park at its base. Covered in 1,000 trees and 20,000 native Australian plants, each residence has been carefully designed to include a terrace with direct access to a tree or its canopy. The project goes further still—its green credentials include a 16,145-square-foot (1,500-square-meter) rooftop solar farm and a gray water recycling system, filtering wastewater to irrigate dense vertical gardens. Locally sourced, low-carbon concrete will be used for the main structure, with recycled and sustainable materials adding warmth and character to public areas. Takada describes the tower as a "benchmark for buildings that make a positive contribution to society and the planet."

→   THE AMBITIOUS SCHEME INVOLVES A LANDSCAPED PUBLIC PARK AT THE BASE
      OF THE TOWER.

↑   THE DIVERSE RANGE OF PLANTS
     CREATES SEASONAL VARIATIONS
     IN COLOR AND GUARANTEES
     YEAR-ROUND FOLIAGE.

↗   THE TOWER WILL BE A RADICAL NEW
     ADDITION TO BRISBANE'S SKYLINE AND
     A SYMBOL FOR SUSTAINABLE VALUES.

→   CURVED BALCONIES REFLECT THE
     ORGANIC FORMS OF THE OVERFLOWING
     PLANTING AND CREATE A SOFTER
     STRUCTURAL PROFILE.

Mille Arbres

OXO Architects and Sou Fujimoto Architects

PARIS, FRANCE

By creating an entirely new ecosystem, Paris's Mille Arbres promises to break new ground in our urban reconnection with nature. OXO and Fujimoto collaborated on the project, proposing an undulating form that contains two layers of forest: a lower public park and an expansive rooftop garden. As its name suggests, 1,000 trees have been carefully selected to encourage biodiversity at a level normally unseen in cities. With the design bridging a busy ring road that marks the administrative boundary of the city, these will also form an essential barrier against chemical and noise pollution. Scheduled for completion in 2023, the scheme includes housing, offices, retail units, and a hotel, as well as a bus station and kindergarten. By imagining architecture that supports diverse human and plant ecosystems, Mille Arbres symbolizes the hopeful resilience of our urban relationship with the environment.

→   A VISUALIZATION OF THE FINISHED DESIGN, DEMONSTRATING THE SCALE
    OF ITS URBAN FOREST.

← AT THE BASE OF THE BUILDING IS AN AMPHITHEATER, GRANTING ACCESS TO THE NEW PUBLIC PARK.

↘ THE LANDSCAPING INCORPORATES SKYLIGHTS, CHANNELING DAYLIGHT INTO THE STRUCTURE.

↓ SEEN FROM ABOVE, THE DESIGN STRADDLES A BUSY RING ON THE OUTSKIRTS OF PARIS.

CUISINE COMMUNE

CHAMBRE D'HÔTES

RESTAURANT

SERRE

← BY FREEING THE PARK FROM GROUND
   LEVEL, THE DESIGN IS ABLE TO USE
   THE SITE FOR MULTIPLE PUBLIC USES.

↑ THE UPPER GARDEN FEATURES A
   VILLAGE OF PITCHED ROOF STRUC-
   TURES, FROM WHICH TO EXPLORE THE
   SURREAL PANORAMA.

→ A DIAGRAM SHOWING THE DISTINCT
   LAYERS OF THE DESIGN, WITH PUBLIC
   ACCESS AND PLANTING ACROSS
   MULTIPLE LEVELS.

Bosco
Verticale

Stefano Boeri Architetti

MILAN, ITALY

↑   STAGGERED BALCONIES ACCOMMODATE 800 TREES FROM MULTIPLE SPECIES, GIVING
    A VARIED TEXTURE TO THE HIGH-RISE FACADES.
→   THE TOWERS HAVE BECOME AN ICONIC PRESENCE IN THE MILANESE SKYLINE, AND
    SYMBOLIC OF A GREENER URBAN FUTURE.

Representing a new urban habitat, Bosco Verticale (or Vertical Forest) is a
pioneering prototype for the future of green housing. Two towers measuring
262 and 367 feet (80 and 112 meters) in height support almost 800 trees and
thousands of shrubs, creating a lush and diverse facade. This impressive
artificial forest is equivalent to 323,000 square feet (30,000 square meters)
of woodland, condensed into a 32,000-square-feet (3,000-square-meter)
footprint. Each building was designed to feature staggered, overhanging
balconies, accommodating large tubs of vegetation and allowing for the
continued growth of the maturing trees. The ambitious project demanded the
slow and careful cultivation of plants in conditions emulating their eventual
high-rise setting. The seasonal transformation of each variety was also
considered, ensuring year-round greenery. The completed towers have
become an icon of sustainability for the city of Milan and are inspiring urban
residences that integrate nature around the world.

← THE TREES USED IN THE PROJECT WERE
  CULTIVATED OVER A LONG PERIOD,
  ALLOWING THEM TO ADJUST TO THE
  MORE INTENSE HIGH-RISE CONDITIONS.

↑ THE PLACEMENT OF THE TREES ALLOWS
  FOR FUTURE GROWTH OF THEIR CANOPIES,
  AS WELL AS RESIDENTS' ENJOYMENT OF
  THE FOLIAGE AT EVERY LEVEL.

→ THE PLANTING IS CAREFULLY MAINTAINED
  BY SPECIALIST GARDENERS WHO RAPPEL
  DOWN THE BUILDING.

The Farmhouse

Precht

CONCEPT

Fei and Chris Precht have envisioned the integration of nature, food production, and sustainable high-rise living. Their imaginative proposal combines an urban farm with a city block, using adaptable triangular modules made from cross-laminated timber (CLT)—a material with a lighter overall environmental footprint than steel, cement, or concrete. With walls comprised of multiple layers— including a scaffold for planting and irrigation systems—these units can be stacked into different configurations to create living, gardening, and shared spaces. Theoretically, structures can be built as high as local regulations allow (providing there is also modification to their thickness). Planting is not confined to the building's exterior. The shape and angle of the pitched modules allow for gardens to exist alongside living spaces: producing food locally, granting self-sufficiency to residents, and creating a community of farmers that can share or sell their harvests. The architects hope this project could be "a catalyst to reconnect ourselves with the life-cycle of our environment."

↑   STRUCTURALLY EFFICIENT TRIANGULAR MODULES ARE STACKED TO MAXIMIZE ACCESS TO NATURAL LIGHT.

←   THE STRUCTURES CAN THEORETICALLY BE ASSEMBLED AS HIGH AS IS NEEDED, ADAPTING TO EACH SITE AND CONTEXT.

↖   THE TRIANGULAR MODULES HAVE A PITCHED ROOF,
    CREATING A SENSE OF SPACE ABOVE.

↑   ANGLED WINDOWS ON THE SIDES OF THE UNITS
    ALLOW FOR VIEWS OF NEIGHBORING GARDENS.

←   A BEDROOM BENEFITING FROM NATURAL LIGHT AND
    A SPECTACULAR HIGH-RISE OUTLOOK.

→   A SHELTERED GARDEN BETWEEN HABITABLE
    MODULES, DESIGNED TO PRODUCE A LOCAL HARVEST
    OF FRUIT AND VEGETABLES.

↑ THE ARCHITECTS HOPE THAT SHARED GARDENS WILL FOSTER A COMMUNITY WITH GREATER AWARENESS OF FOOD PRODUCTION.

→ THE PROFILE OF THE TOWER IS SOFTENED BY OPEN TRELLISES AND PLANTING.

EDEN

↑ LAYERED BALCONIES HOUSE A CASCADE OF FLORA, SEEN HERE FROM ABOVE.

→ THE ORGANIC, SHELL-SHAPED PLANTERS ARE SCALED DOWN AS THEY APPROACH THE
   GROUND LEVEL GARDEN, CONNECTING WITH A HUMAN SENSE OF SCALE.

Heatherwick Studio

SINGAPORE

Located in the historic residential district of Newton, Heatherwick Studio has reimagined the typical glass and steel tower. The core concept of their design was to create homes embedded within lush gardens, while retaining the benefits of high-rise living: privacy, light, and views of the cityscape. The lowest of the building's generous apartments are 88 feet (27 meters) above the base of the structure: an area dedicated to a dense tropical garden. This allows each residence to benefit from natural cross ventilation and to be cooled without artificial climate controls. The project's use of glass was also minimized, with windows set back into the tower's concrete facade—further reducing solar gain. Central living spaces are surrounded by smaller private rooms and organic, shell-shaped balconies. These balconies, made from polished concrete, act as giant planters for abundant foliage, with space for further growth over the building's lifetime. The resulting green cascades, overflowing from numerous petal-like forms, offer a romantic vision of modern Eden.

←   THE OVERFLOWING PLANTERS FORM A LUSH WATERFALL OF GREENERY BETWEEN THE MORE STRUCTURAL FACETS OF THE TOWER.

↓   VIEWED FROM GROUND LEVEL, THE STAGGERED POSITIONING OF THE PLANTERS CREATES VISUAL INTRIGUE AND BREAKS UP THE BUILDING'S LINEARITY.

↑   EACH APARTMENT HAS VIEWS ACROSS
     THE CITY, FRAMED BY TROPICAL FOLIAGE
     AND A GENEROUS CURVED BALCONY.

↗   THE RUGGED CONCRETE OF THE FACADE
     CONTRASTS WITH THE SMOOTH
     UNDERSIDE OF THE CANTILEVERED
     PLANTERS.

→   THE NATURAL FORMS OF THE COURT-
     YARD'S PLANTING ARE ECHOED BY THE
     CURVES OF HEATHERWICK STUDIO'S
     TRADEMARK SPUN CHAIR.

1000 Trees

Heatherwick Studio

SHANGHAI, CHINA

Reminiscent of a pixelated mountain, Heatherwick Studio has designed a multi-use complex within a new form of urban topography. Proposed as a phased development of two such mountains, built on neighboring sites near the city's M50 arts district, this staggered artificial landscape rises from the banks of the Wusong River and houses hotels, shops, and offices. Its structural columns are reinvented as prominent, stem-like planters, containing a diverse population of thousands of trees and plants that cover the exterior. Selected from native Chinese varieties, their considered planting achieves variation in color, size, and even smell. Designed in alternating stripes of gray and green granite, the building's facade nods to the layered structure of sedimentary rock formations. Giant interior atriums maximize natural light, and the first mountain's undulating form is sliced flat on the southern side—a canvas for local and international artists, as though excavation has revealed a vibrant inner life. The resulting design is miles away from a traditional, monolithic block, retaining and developing an eye-catching dialogue with the landscape and urban environment.

↑   THE DESIGN UNDULATES LIKE A TREE-TOPPED MOUNTAIN—A GREEN REPRIEVE WITHIN THIS DENSE URBAN SPRAWL.

25 Verde

Luciano Pia

TURIN, ITALY

↑ THE CENTRAL COURTYARD OF 25 VERDE, PLANTED WITH 50 TREES, ACTS AS THE LUNGS OF THE PROJECT.

→ THE DESIGN'S OTHERWORLDLY TANGLE OF WOOD, STEEL, AND TREES, AS SEEN FROM THE STREETS OF TURIN.

25 Verde is a glorious insight into Luciano Pia's imagination—a vision of treetop living, made reality in the city. Man-made materials and nature sit side-by-side, a tangle of terraces and trees supported by steel trunks that grow from the sidewalk. The project combines 63 homes with a lush forest of more than 200 trees. Inhabitants can observe the changing seasons from homes clad in naturally weathered larch shingles. At the heart of the plan sits a generous courtyard garden, acting as the project's lungs—producing oxygen while filtering pollution and absorbing harmful compounds. The site's combined greenery also creates a microclimate that mediates seasonal temperature change. The addition of a geothermal heat pump, plus a rainwater recycling system for plant irrigation, complete a highly sustainable development. The joy of this project lies in its unique irregularity: just as in a real forest, there are unexpected shapes and collisions that allow for new discoveries from every angle.

← THE STEEL SUPPORTS RESEMBLE
TREE TRUNKS, GROWING FROM
THE GROUND TO SUPPORT TREE
HOUSE-LIKE HOMES ABOVE.

↑ METAL PLANTERS CONTAIN
TREES OF VARYING HEIGHTS
AND SPECIES, WITH SEASONAL
FOLIAGE SELECTED FOR THE
NEEDS OF EACH LOCATION.

→ LARCH SHINGLES PROVIDE A
NATURAL FACADE, CAPABLE OF
WRAPPING AROUND THE ORGANIC
CURVES OF PIA'S DESIGN.

Second Home Hollywood

SelgasCano

LOS ANGELES, CA, USA

A bold contrast to the corporate office cubicle, SelgasCano makes jungle workspaces an attractive reality. In their latest collaboration with the innovative coworking company Second Home, the architects created a fantastical oasis for this Hollywood campus. Known for their bold use of color, SelgasCano filled the site with 60 sun-yellow oval pods, each offering a 360-degree view of nature. A former parking lot was dramatically rewilded with 10,000 plants and trees, establishing a diverse local ecosystem. The pods draw in fresh air from these leafy surroundings, enriching lively areas of focus and creativity. Anne Banning Community House—designed in the sixties by architect Paul Revere Williams—sits within the scheme and was renovated to house additional work areas, common amenities, and a lush, tree-filled courtyard. Combined with Second Home's enviable program of wellness events and public lectures, this project sets a new standard in green workspaces.

↑   ONE OF THE FUTURISTIC WORKSPACE PODS, WITH TRANSPARENT, CURVED WALLS OVERLOOKING THE GARDEN.

→   ANNE BANNING COMMUNITY HOUSE HAS BEEN TRANSFORMED INTO AN OASIS, CONTAINING ADDITIONAL WORKING AND EVENTS SPACES.

↓   BETWEEN THE PODS, MEANDERING PATHS AND LANDSCAPING PROVIDE AREAS FOR REST AND INTERACTION.

← 60 OVAL PODS AND EXTENSIVE REWILDING TRANSFORM THE FORMER PARKING LOT.
↘ SHARED SPACES AROUND THE CAMPUS HOST MULTIPLE EVENTS AS PART OF SECOND HOME'S PUBLIC PROGRAM.
↓ THE CENTRAL COURTYARD OF ANNE BANNING COMMUNITY HOUSE IS FILLED WITH TREES AND LUSH GREENERY.

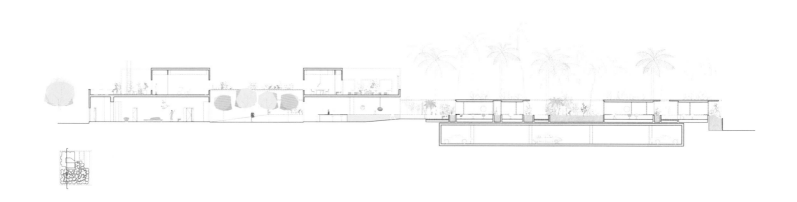

↑   THE PODS' PROXIMITY CREATES A FEELING
OF COMMUNITY AND SHELTER, BUT STILL
ALLOWS PLANTS TO THRIVE IN BETWEEN.

↖   AS SHOWN BY THIS SECTION DRAWING,
PARTIAL BURIAL OF THE PODS IN THE
SURROUNDING PLANTER BEDS IMPROVES
THEIR INSULATION.

→   THE STATEMENT-MAKING, SUNNY YELLOW
OF THE POD ROOFS IS A PUNCHY ADDITION
TO THIS LARGELY MONOCHROME CONTEXT.

Maggie's Leeds

Heatherwick Studio

LEEDS, U.K.

As the 26th Maggie's center, this peaceful and restorative scheme harnesses the curative benefits of greenery to create a place of healing. Founded in 1995, Maggie's is a charity that has transformed cancer treatment through their international network of sites. As well as offering free practical and emotional support to patients, their family, and friends, each location provides a space away from sterile hospital environments—and opportunities to enjoy daily life while dealing with serious illness. Heatherwick Studio's design is arranged around three planter-like forms that contain counseling rooms, and flare out to support a multilevel green roof planted with native English species. Soaring glass panels allow for views of a lush, landscaped garden, despite the inner-city location. The multidisciplinary practice also designed bespoke furniture and custom details that further transform the building. By incorporating nature throughout, this architecture encourages intimate connection and emotional release.

→ NESTLED INTO THE LUSH GARDEN, THE BUILDING EMITS A WARM AND INVITING GLOW AT DUSK.

→   FREE FROM HARD PARTITIONS, COMMUNAL SPACES FLOW BETWEEN SCULPTURAL TIMBER PILLARS.

↓   NATURAL MATERIALS, WARM LIGHTING, AND GENEROUS PLANTING HELP CREATE AN IMMEDIATELY REASSURING ENVIRONMENT.

Jungalow

↑   THE CENTRAL ATRIUM FEATURES A ROOFTOP OCULUS AND TRELLIS TO CULTIVATE A WALL OF GREENERY.

→   THE SOUTHERN FACADE OF THE BUILDING, WITH A TERRACE AND ENTRANCE INTO THE HOME.

Neogenesis+Studi0261

SURAT, INDIA

Designed for an agriculturist and his family as a lush sanctuary from the urban sprawl of Surat, a city on India's west coast, this home invites the garden inside. A central core of greenery in the form of a three-story atrium, filled with cascading plants and natural light, creates a verdant interior around which the spaces of the home are organized. One side of the atrium features an open trellis, allowing vines to climb the full height of the building. At ground level, a retractable glass screen separates the planting from an open-plan living and dining area—allowing this boundary to be dissolved entirely—while on the uppermost floor, round windows frame views of the internal garden. Topped with a circular opening, the atrium's dramatic oculus provides an overhead focal point. By consciously keeping the building's materials muted, the architects direct focus toward nature in this home, offering a simple but compelling vision of garden living.

←   THE HEIGHT OF THE ATRIUM ALLOWS MULTIPLE LEVELS OF THE HOME TO BENEFIT FROM VIEWS OF GREENERY AND AN IMPROVED QUALITY OF LIGHT.

↘   ON THE GROUND FLOOR, A GLASS PARTITION CAN BE FOLDED AWAY—MAKING THE INNER GARDEN AN EXTENSION OF THE LIVING AREA.

↓   A PORTHOLE WINDOW IN THE UPSTAIRS BEDROOM FRAMES GLIMPSES OF THE CENTRAL ATRIUM AND ITS PLANTING.

A Brutalist Tropical Home in Bali

Patisandhika and Daniel Mitchell

BALI, INDONESIA

↑ THE THRESHOLD TO THE DRAMATIC, DOUBLE-HEIGHT LIVING AREA OF THIS LUXURIOUS HOME.

→ PLANTED WITH SHADE-GIVING PALM TREES, A GEOMETRIC TERRACE CANTILEVERS OVER THE GARDEN.

Located in a small valley on Bali's southern coast, this geometric concrete home was designed as a collaboration between architectural studio Patisandhika and multidisciplinary designer Daniel Mitchell. Inspired by the American architect Ray Kappe, the L-shaped structure blurs the divide between the indoors and outdoors. It creates a series of changing moods through a dynamic layout and material selection. A composition of exaggerated concrete slabs and fins with deep overhangs create shade and coolness in an impressive double-height living space at the center of the building. Rough expanses of concrete contrast with warm wood accents, enhancing the site's deliberately wild landscaping. Rooftop solar panels and a rainwater collection system were key to ensuring the sustainability of the house, which endeavors to merge with its environment. With time, the surrounding tangle of greenery will overgrow the interior, embedding the building in its lush tropical setting.

↑   INFLUENCED BY THE ARCHITECTURE OF RAY KAPPE, THE INTERIOR INCORPORATES POLISHED CONCRETE AND BOLD PRIMARY COLORS.

→   PLANTING INSIDE AND OUTSIDE THE HOME CREATES FLOWING SPACES AND BLURRED THRESHOLDS.

→   DEEP CONCRETE LINTELS ARE DESIGNED TO CREATE COOL INTERNAL SPACES, CONNECTED WITH THE SURROUNDINGS.
↓   LOCALLY ABUNDANT NATURAL MATERIALS ARE USED TO SHADE THE HOUSE.

Casa Carmen

OA+M Arquitectos

MEDELLÍN, COLOMBIA

Designed by Medellín-based studio OA+M Arquitectos, this high-altitude residence was designed to wrap around sheltered gardens and integrate nature into its inhabitants' daily lives. The luxurious structure is built in a Z-shape, creating spaces protected from the wind and chillier temperatures, and maximizing every room's contact with the surrounding landscape. In addition to its gardens, nature is brought into the very heart of the home: planter beds frame circulation spaces, as though growing through the full-height windows. Constructed using red adobe brick, concrete, and wood, the architects chose natural materials that would subtly weather and mature over the life of the building. Their intention was to create a house that would maintain connection with the outdoors, particularly the nearby nature reserve. This is forged not only through its flowing plan—following a path that leads to the forest beyond—but also by its continuous green roof, blending the design into the hillside. The result is a home deeply entwined with its setting.

↑   SEEN IN ITS HIGH-ALTITUDE CONTEXT, THE Z-SHAPED HOME INCORPORATES A CONTINUOUS GREEN ROOF.

↑   SET INTO THE FLOORING, INTERIOR
    BEDS OF PLANTING EFFECTIVELY BLUR
    THE THRESHOLD BETWEEN INDOORS
    AND OUTDOORS.

↗   FLOOR-TO-CEILING WINDOWS OFFER
    UNOBSTRUCTED VIEWS OF NATURE
    THROUGHOUT THE HOME.

→   DARK WOOD WAS APPLIED TO BOTH THE
    INTERIOR AND EXTERIOR OF THE DESIGN.

→   A PLAYFUL STEPPING-STONE BRIDGES AN INDOOR BED OF PLANTING AT THE THRESHOLD OF A ROOM.
↓   THE ARCHITECTS DESIGNED THE SPACES OF THE HOME TO FLOW, WHILE FRAMING VIEWS OF THE LANDSCAPE BEYOND.

House of the Big Arch

Frankie Pappas

WATERBERG BIOSPHERE RESERVE, LIMPOPO
PROVINCE, SOUTH AFRICA

↑   THE HOUSE IS NESTLED DEEP WITHIN THE MATURE FOREST OF THE WATERBERG
NATURE RESERVE.

→   THE INCREDIBLY NARROW PROFILE OF THE BUILDING PREVENTED THE FELLING OF
EVEN A SINGLE TREE.

On this unique site located within the South African Waterberg nature reserve, the Frankie Pappas collective's guiding principle was simple: do the forest no harm. Their design threads the narrow house between the trees, allowing the project to avoid all felling and to sit within established leaf canopies. This unusual home is composed of dynamic brick forms and timber bridges, organized around a central 11-foot-wide (3-meter-wide) spine to create intriguing internal and external spaces. Far from feeling cramped, the skinny structure benefits from generous ceiling heights and picture windows looking out onto the surrounding greenery. Its considered sequence of spaces ends in a terrace supported by a brick arch—after which the house is named—with a rough, stock brick column echoing the surrounding tree trunks. As the remote location is not connected to electricity or water networks, the roof of this vision of off-grid living houses solar panels and a water collection system.

↑   A WIDE TERRACE, SUPPORTED BY A BRICK ARCH, CREATES AN OUTDOOR LIVING ROOM IMMERSED IN THE NATURAL BEAUTY OF THE RESERVE.

→   THE CONSTRAINTS OF THE FORESTED SITE BECAME A FEATURE OF ITS DESIGN—AS WITH THIS SLENDER FRONT ENTRANCE.

↖ THE ARCHITECT'S SKETCH SHOWS HOW THE BUILDING IS NESTLED IN AMONG THE TREES.

← DESPITE THE HOME'S NARROW FOOTPRINT, THE INTERIOR FEELS SPACIOUS AND CONNECTED TO THE SURROUNDING LANDSCAPE.

↓ AN INTERIOR VIEW OF THE BRICK STRUCTURE AND ADJOINING OUTDOOR SPACES.

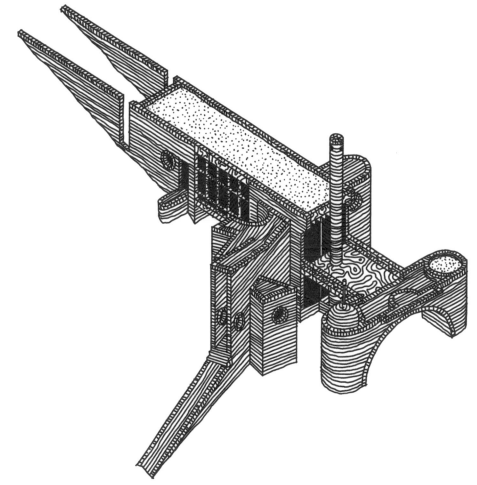

←   A BRIDGE MADE OF WOOD AND
      GLASS CONNECTS THE SPACES
      OF THE MAIN LIVING AREA WITH
      THE OUTDOOR TERRACE.

↑   THE GREEN ROOF ON THE MAIN VOLUME
      OF THE STRUCTURE BLENDS THE
      BUILDING INTO THE CANOPY.

→   A SKETCH OF THE COLLECTIVE'S VISION,
      SHOWING GEOMETRIC BRICK FORMS
      NEGOTIATING THE RESTRICTED,
      SLOPING SITE.

Mạo Khê House

HGAA

MẠO KHÊ, QUẢNG NINH PROVINCE, VIETNAM

HGAA has gained a reputation in Vietnam for subtly integrating architecture and nature, and this project further proves that flair. Built on a square site, the U-shaped home surrounds a courtyard containing mature trees and a large pond. Also known as the Greenery Curtain House, the periphery of the building is planted with hanging vines, granting privacy to its inhabitants and shielding floor-to-ceiling windows from solar gain. The result is a stunning radial design that maximizes the relatively small surrounding garden and offers views of greenery from every room in the house. Stone flooring runs from the interior to the outdoors, reinforcing a sense of living inseparably with and among nature. On the second floor, two terraces create the space for a pair of vegetable gardens. These are connected by a reading room with low windows, looking down onto the courtyard below.

→ THE CENTRAL COURTYARD OF THE HOUSE, WITH A KOI POND AND BORDERED BY HANGING VINES.

↑   THE CURTAIN OF FOLIAGE IN THE CENTRAL GARDEN CREATES LAYERS OF SPACE, AND PERSPECTIVES WITH DEPTH AND INTRIGUE.

→   LIT BY A GENEROUS SKYLIGHT, VIEWS FROM THE READING ROOM ON THE UPPER FLOOR ARE DIRECTED TOWARD THE COURTYARD BELOW.

← WALKWAYS NAVIGATE THE FULL HEIGHT OF THE STRUCTURE, ENABLING PUBLIC ACCESS TO THE ROOFTOP GARDENS.
↓ THE WINDOWS ARE SET BACK, CREATING SHADED BALCONIES FILLED WITH PLANTS THAT OFFER ADDITIONAL, INTIMATE GREEN SPACES.

→   THE SIMPLE BRICK FORMS OF THE HOUSE ARE SOFTENED BY A FRINGE OF TRAILING VINES.
↓   TERRACES ON THE SECOND FLOOR PROVIDE SPACE FOR PRODUCTIVE VEGETABLE GARDENS, DISTINCT FROM THE ORNAMENTAL
     COURTYARD BELOW.

The Red Roof

TAA Design

QUẢNG NGÃI, VIETNAM

Located in a rapidly developing coastal province, this creative design brings nature and community into the heart of a compact Vietnamese home. Tiled and plastered in bold terra-cotta red, the building's main feature is a unique stepped garden on its low, sloping roof. Planters grow vegetables for the local community, enabling self-sufficiency, and offering a lush, eye-catching contrast to the earthy red of the exterior. Internal courtyards of varying heights are subtly integrated with indoor spaces, creating adaptable spaces for multifunctional use. At the front of the building, a covered bicycle repair area faces the village's main road, encouraging connection with the neighborhood. Undeniably beautiful, TAA Design's scheme is all the more impressive for its integration of nature with the functional demands of daily life. This home foregrounds the needs of a working family and community, establishing a nourishing coexistence between its inhabitants and the garden.

→   THE COMMUNITY ROOF GARDEN, HOUSED BY A SERIES OF STEPPED PLANTERS.

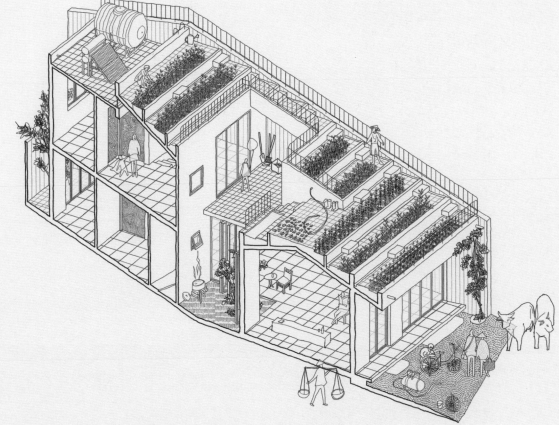

← COURTYARDS AND TERRACES OFFER
  OUTDOOR AREAS FOR DOMESTIC TASKS
  AND RELAXATION, SEPARATE TO THE
  ROOF GARDEN.

↑ THE CONTRASTING RED AND GREEN
  STRIPES OF THE TILES AND PLANTING
  ARE AN EYE-CATCHING COMBINATION.

→ CUTTING THROUGH THE HOUSE, THIS
  SECTION DRAWING ILLUSTRATES THE
  INTEGRATION OF EVERYDAY LIFE,
  COMMUNITY, AND PLANTS.

Brick Cave

H&P Architects

HANOI, VIETNAM

This project uses bold, sculptural forms to create an ideal habitat—sheltered from the extremes of Hanoi's climate—for plants and humans alike. Two brick walls envelope the building like a protective skin, establishing an atrium that blurs the threshold between interior and exterior, and creating a cool microclimate for the home within. Constructed using widely spaced bricks and metal lattice panels, the architects maintained connection to street level and privacy to the upper floor. At a height of 6.5 feet (2 meters) the brick wall slopes inwards, minimizing the impact of the house's mass on the neighborhood, and covering the atrium space in a dappled shade, like a tree's foliage. Inside the home, carefully curated openings frame views of vegetation with the perforated surfaces behind, maximizing the select landscaping and natural light. As the name Brick Cave suggests, this in-between space full of greenery feels atmospheric and introduces a place in the home in which to coexist with nature.

→   THE DESIGN ACHIEVES A MIXTURE OF SUNNY AND SHADED SPACES, INCLUDING A THRIVING GARDEN AND COOL LIVING AREAS.

↑   THE ROOFTOP VEGETABLE GARDEN OFFERS A SUSTAINABLE SOURCE OF FOOD FOR THE INHABITANTS OF THE HOME.

→   ANGLING BACK THE BUILDING'S FORM SOFTENS THE SCALE OF THE STRUCTURE AND ALLOWS MORE LIGHT TO REACH GROUND LEVEL.

← THE WALLED SPACE BETWEEN THE STREET AND THE HOME CREATES A DOUBLE-HEIGHT ATRIUM, TO BE FILLED OVER TIME BY PLANTING.

↓ WIDELY SPACED BRICKWORK FILTERS INTENSE SUNLIGHT, ILLUMINATING THE ATRIUM AND FURTHER INTO THE HOME.

Ha House

Located in a dense residential neighborhood in Ho Chi Minh City, VTN Architects has made inventive use of a tight urban plot. Stacked rooms are linked by stepped, verdant gardens and a series of angular terraces, creating the feeling of a treehouse in the city. Built for a multigenerational family, this continual greenery provides both private and shared spaces for relaxation, socializing, and play. Planting was designed to offer privacy, as well as shielding living areas from the city's intense heat. With the narrow site flanked by neighboring houses, available sunlight comes at a premium. By setting back and twisting the volume of the building as it rises, the architects have achieved intriguing depth, air flow, and multiple opportunities for windows and skylights. Mainly constructed using wood and locally sourced brick—lowering the project's financial cost and carbon footprint—the resulting warm palette creates an inviting and cozy interior.

VTN Architects

HO CHI MINH CITY, VIETNAM

→   LAYERS OF SHELTERED TERRACES PROVIDE EXTRA LIVING SPACE AND OPPORTUNITIES TO ENJOY THE LUSH PLANTING.

↓   POSITIONED TO DRAW LINES OF SIGHT BETWEEN MULTIPLE SPACES OF THE HOME, THE TERRACES MAINTAIN A SOCIAL FAMILY DYNAMIC.

↑   THE INTERIOR INFORMS THE MATERIALITY
OF THE EXTERIOR, ACHIEVING HARMONIOUS
TRANSITIONS BETWEEN WOOD AND BRICK.

←   THE BUILDING IS CROWNED BY A TILED
ROOFTOP TERRACE, HOUSING BEDS
OF PLANTING AND OVERLOOKING THE
SPACES BENEATH.

→   THE ARCHITECTS' DRAWINGS EMPHASIZE
THEIR INTENTION TO THREAD GARDENS
THROUGHOUT THE STRUCTURE.

Wall House

CTA Creative Architects

BIÊN HÒA, ĐỒNG NAI PROVINCE, VIETNAM

Imagining this project, the client and architects wanted to provide healthier indoor air quality for a multigenerational family. Their driving concept was a building that could breathe. In order to achieve this, the architects designed a unique facade made from stacked, hollow bricks. Salvaged from nearby building sites and rotated to expose preexisting perforations in their structure, they cast a dappled, natural light and allow air to circulate freely. Leafy planting further improves air quality and melds the garden and the home. This porous boundary creates semi-outdoor shared spaces, topped with a glass roof, in which the family have their main social and living areas. Eight separate blocks, spaced around the communal center—yet linked by the breathing walls—contain private rooms. In their clever execution of a strong, simple idea, CTA Creative Architects have achieved a beautiful home with a remarkably organic quality.

→   AS DAYLIGHT PASSES OVER THE RECLAIMED BRICKWORK, IT CREATES AN ANIMATED AND TEXTURED FACADE.

↗ ON THE GROUND FLOOR, A LIGHTWEIGHT
STAIRCASE HOVERS OVER BEDS
OF PLANTING.

→ PART OF THE SEMI-OUTDOOR LIVING
SPACE BETWEEN THE OUTER WALL AND
MORE PRIVATE AREAS OF THE HOME.

↓ THE COMMUNAL COURTYARD IS FILLED
WITH NATURAL LIGHT THAT ENTERS
THROUGH THE GLASS ROOF.

→   EVEN WHEN THE ENTRANCE IS CLOSED, THE BUILDING MAINTAINS A PERMEABLE RELATIONSHIP WITH THE OUTSIDE WORLD.

↘   BY KEEPING THE KITCHEN OPEN TO THE CENTRAL COURTYARD, THE DESIGN DEEPENS RESIDENTS' CONNECTION WITH THE OUTDOORS.

↓   THE POROUS BRICK WALLS INTRODUCE FLASHES OF LIGHT AND COLOR TO THE INTERIOR, CAST BY THE GREENERY BEYOND.

1000   5000   10000

← VIEWED FROM OUTSIDE, THE
   BUILDING'S BOX-LIKE FORM AND
   TEXTURED WALLS SPARK CURIOSITY.

↑ TO THE REAR OF THE HOME, A GARDEN
   OF MATURE TREES PROVIDES AN
   ADDITIONAL GREEN SPACE FOR THE
   GROWING FAMILY.

→ A SECTION DRAWING SHOWING THE
   ELEMENTS OF THE DESIGN, WRAPPED
   BY THE BRICK WALL AND FILLED
   WITH PLANTS.

Cornwall Gardens

CHANG Architects

SINGAPORE

In this design for an ambitious private home, CHANG Architects creates cohesive communal spaces focused on greenery and nature, while offering privacy for a multigenerational family. This extraordinary, U-shaped building wraps around an expansive central courtyard with a generous swimming pool. Private rooms are arranged along the periphery, screened by cascading vines and planter boxes full of tropical vegetation. The resulting spaces are completely surrounded by greenery, filtering strong sunlight as well as air and noise pollution. At roof level, the architects designed a stepped garden which covers the entirety of the home and includes rainwater collection tanks for irrigation. The ziggurat form of these rooftop planters echoes a hilly landscape. Upon entering the house, a smaller courtyard containing a waterfall and koi pond at basement level leave a striking impression, with metal mesh walkways overhead, covered in passion fruit vines to complete a secluded tropical oasis.

→   THE CENTRAL COURTYARD OF THE HOME, FEATURING A SWIMMING POOL
     SURROUNDING A SUNKEN SEATING AREA.

← STEPPED PLANTERS ON THE ROOF CREATE THE SPACE FOR A TIERED GARDEN.

↘ THE BUILDING AS SEEN FROM THE STREET, WITH A FACADE PACKED WITH CHARCOAL LOGS THAT FILTER NOISE AND AIR POLLUTION.

↓ THE SMALLER COURTYARD WITHIN THE ENTRANCE TO THE HOME, CONTAINING A WATERFALL AND KOI POND, SURROUNDED BY CASCADING PLANTS.

↑ OVERLOOKING THE CENTRAL COURTYARD,
THE UPPER FLOOR BEDROOMS ARE
SCREENED BY HANGING VINES WHILE
REMAINING OPEN TO THE FRESH AIR.

↗ THE VIEW OF THE LANDSCAPED
COURTYARD AND ROOF GARDEN FROM
A BEDROOM.

→ ONE SIDE OF THE COURTYARD CONTAINS
A GROUND FLOOR AREA FOR DINING
AND SOCIALIZING.

→ ON ENTERING THE HOUSE, VISITORS ARE GREETED BY THIS SMALL, LUSH COURTYARD AND THE SOUND OF A WATERFALL.

↓ PASSION FRUIT VINES SHADE A WALKWAY AND OFFER PRIVACY.

Weekend House in São Paulo

SPBR Arquitetos

SÃO PAULO, BRAZIL

To avoid their congested weekend commute to the beach, this project's clients set an interesting challenge: to bring that retreat to downtown São Paulo. On a tight urban plot, the architects designed the ground floor to be as construction-free as possible, maximizing space for a secluded walled garden with ponds. Upstairs, private living areas are connected by lightweight galvanized staircases, while the roof terrace features a generous pool and solarium that offer a panoramic view of the city. Placing the pool on the roof—rather than at ground level—allows the water to be warmed by the sun, as well as structurally balancing the weight of the building. The architects wanted to give the impression of bathing in a water tower—making for a kind of urban beach. By prioritizing outdoor space throughout the design of the house, SPBR transforms an otherwise shady plot into the perfect weekend retreat.

→　THE LANDSCAPING OF THE GARDEN TRANSFORMS THE STRUCTURAL ELEMENTS OF THE BUILDING INTO FEATURES AND
　　FOCAL POINTS.
↘　THE HOUSE IS SUPPORTED AT GROUND LEVEL BY CONCRETE COLUMNS—CREATING MAXIMUM SPACE FOR PLANTING AND A POND.
↓　THE ROOFTOP IS ACCESSED VIA A DRAMATIC CENTRAL STAIRCASE, RUNNING FROM GROUND LEVEL.

Welcome to the Jungle House

CplusC Architectural Workshop

SYDNEY, AUSTRALIA

Welcome to the Jungle House is not only a carefully considered family home—it is an experiment in sustainable living. Inspired by a famous Le Corbusier quote, the architects conceived the house to be "a machine for sustaining life." Home to the studio's director and his family, every inch has been designed for adaptability and daily life, while keeping its ecological impact firmly in sight. CplusC went as far as to think about the full life cycle of the building in their sustainability decisions—for example, selecting materials that can be reused in the future. Solar panels cover one side of the building, freeing up space on the roof for an ambitious aquaponic garden of native plants, fruit, and vegetables. Plant beds are irrigated using nutrient-rich water from an open-air fishpond, inhabited by edible silver perch. Every architectural element strives to counter the detachment between food sources, ecosystems, and our urban lives, encouraging a lasting lifestyle change.

→   BEFORE THE WELCOME TO THE JUNGLE HOUSE, THIS URBAN PLOT WAS PREVIOUSLY OCCUPIED BY A TWO-STORY STRUCTURE THAT WAS CLOSE TO COLLAPSE.

↘   THE HOME'S UNIQUE APPROACH TO VENTILATION IS SEEN FROM THE BEDROOM.

↓   THE HOUSE'S ORIGINAL WINDOWS ARE FRAMED IN PRE-RUSTED STEEL, WITH NEWLY ADDED OPENINGS FRAMED IN WHITE POWDER-COATED STEEL.

→ LOUVERS SHIELD THE HOME FROM
   DIRECT SOLAR GAIN AND HELP TO KEEP
   THE INTERIOR AT A COMFORTABLE
   TEMPERATURE.

→ RETHINKING THE INHABITANTS'
   RELATIONSHIP TO NATURE WITHIN
   THEIR EVERYDAY LIVING SPACE WAS
   KEY TO THE BUILDING'S CONCEPT.

↓ ARCHITECTURAL ELEMENTS WERE
   DESIGNED WITH THEIR FUTURE
   DECONSTRUCTION AND SUSTAINABLE
   REUSE IN MIND.

Planter Box House

Formzero

KUALA LUMPUR, MALAYSIA

↑   THE MULTIPLE LAYERS OF PLANTER BOXES AND TERRACES AT THE FRONT OF THE HOME—AS SEEN FROM ABOVE.

→   VIEWED FROM THE STREET, THE STACKED FORMS CREATE A STRIKING COMPOSITION OF CONCRETE AND PLANTS.

The stacked containers of Planter Box House, overflowing with lush greenery, make quite a statement in a Kuala Lumpur neighborhood dominated by red tile roofs. Designed as a home for a retired couple with an interest in urban farming and self-sufficiency, a playful cluster of textured boxes creates generous terraces and the space for over 40 types of edible plants. The architects were inspired by readily available local materials, particularly split bamboo panels—a craft of the indigenous Temuan people. These panels were used as formwork for the concrete planters, lending a softer, more organic texture to their exterior walls while still feeling distinctly urban. The deep planters also retain stormwater, creating irrigation reservoirs. Additionally, the building is carefully designed to be passively cooled, thus requiring less energy. The true success of this house lies in its integration of living and nature. The spaces oscillate from indoors to outdoors, allowing its inhabitants to live among the plants they cultivate.

←   THE DOUBLE-HEIGHT KITCHEN AND DINING AREA FEATURES FLOOR-TO-CEILING WINDOWS THAT OPEN ONTO A SMALL OUTDOOR YARD.

↓   THE PLANTING THROUGHOUT THE HOME FOCUSES ON EDIBLE VARIETIES THAT THE RESIDENTS CAN HARVEST.

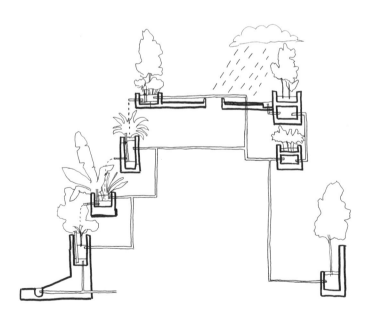

↑   THE LIVING SPACE OPENS ONTO A GENEROUS TERRACE.

←   LUSH VEGETATION SEEN FROM BELOW.

↗   THE ARCHITECT'S SKETCH SHOWS HOW RAINWATER IS DISTRIBUTED THROUGHOUT.

→   THE TRIPLE-HEIGHT LIVING SPACE AND CONNECTING STAIRCASES.

↑   BY INCORPORATING PLANTED TERRACES INTO EVERY LEVEL OF THE DESIGN, EVEN THE MOST INTIMATE ROOMS BENEFIT FROM A GARDEN VIEW.

→   SPLIT BAMBOO FORMWORK GIVES AN ORGANIC TEXTURE TO THE CAST CONCRETE PLANTERS, ECHOING THE NATURAL FORMS OF THE GREENERY.

Green Box

act_romegialli

CERIDO, LOMBARDY, ITALY

Like an undiscovered ruin overgrown with vines, there is a romantic imperfection to act_romegialli's Green Box—making it all the more beautiful. Over time, a cloud of vegetation has covered this renovated building, guided by a pitch roof-shaped support structure that envelops its original stone walls and flat, concrete roof. Using a very limited palette of wood, concrete, and galvanized steel, the design balances the language of industrial and practical spaces with that of a tranquil garden hideaway. At dusk, the glowing interior is visible through the branches, its angular silhouette softened by a tangle of greenery. A mixture of deciduous, annual, and perennial varieties was carefully selected to provide a constant cover of plants and flowers throughout the year. Generous picture windows, shaded by the vegetation, offer views from the building to the garden beyond. The wildness of this design is especially successful: by allowing the architecture to all but disappear, it celebrates the unpredictable beauty of nature.

↑ THE PITCHED ROOF VOLUME OF GREEN BOX, ENGULFED BY A CLOUD OF FOLIAGE AND FLOWERS.

← BREAKING THROUGH THE VEGETATION, THE CHIMNEY IS THE SOLE INDICATION OF THE FUNCTIONAL BUILDING WITHIN.

↓ INSIDE IS A MINIMAL BUT PRACTICAL SPACE, CREATED USING A LIMITED PALETTE OF MATERIALS IN MUTED TONES.

← THE DESIGN HAS BOTH INDUSTRIAL AND
   DOMESTIC QUALITIES, AND THE FEEL OF
   A ROMANTIC RUIN.

↑ THE INTERIOR OF THE BUILDING GLOWS
   THROUGH THE FOLIAGE AT NIGHT—AN
   INVITING NOCTURNAL SHELTER.

→ A DRAWING OF THE MINIMAL STRUCTURE
   OF THE TRELLIS, WHICH SUPPORTS
   CLIMBING, WILD PLANTING.

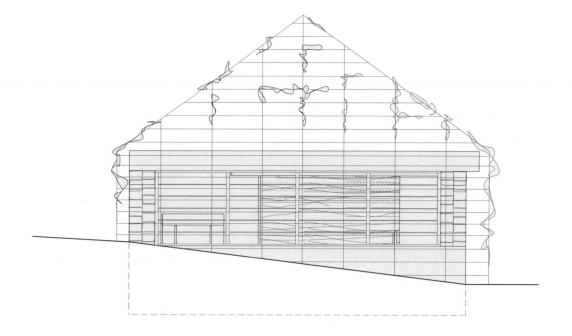

Tennyson 205

Studio Rick Joy

MEXICO CITY, MEXICO

↑   THE HOUSE AS SEEN FROM THE STREET; NEIGHBORING BUILDINGS ON THREE SIDES RESTRICT ITS ACCESS TO LIGHT.

→   LIGHT WELLS SUSTAIN COURTYARD GARDENS WITHIN THE HOME AND CREATE ATMOSPHERIC ATRIUM SPACES.

Rick Joy is known for creating beautiful buildings in wide-open expanses of desert landscape. With this project in Mexico City, he faced the opposite setting—a tight urban plot, surrounded by buildings on three sides. Despite these constraints, Tennyson 205 is a sanctuary that still captures Joy's characteristic openness and appreciation of nature. The primary challenge was creating access to natural light: three generous light wells draw daylight through all five stories, before reaching sheltered gardens below. Ephemeral planting cascades down these channels, contrasting with and softening the roughness of exposed concrete, and providing interior views of greenery. The rugged, quarry-like walls have a very sculptural quality, with deep reveals around openings—as though carved from a cliff face. Through its simple combination of textures and greenery, this urban building takes on the qualities of a timeless landscape—one not built, but rather discovered.

↑   IN THIS URBAN CONTEXT, INTERIOR COURTYARDS GIVE LIVING SPACES A STRONG CONNECTION TO NATURE.

→   SHUTTERED CONCRETE IS USED TO FORM PLANTERS AND SEATING IN SHELTERED ROOMS, OPEN TO THE OUTDOORS.

← PLANTER BOXES SET INTO THE EXTERIOR WALLS OF THE LIGHT WELL CONTAIN TRAILING PLANTS.
↓ COURTYARDS OFFER INTERIOR VIEWS OF GREENERY AND THE SKY, DESPITE A COMPACT SITE.

↑ INTERIOR SPACES ARE LIT THROUGH THE
  PLANT-FILLED LIGHT WELL.

← A BATHROOM'S LARGE WINDOWS OPEN
  ONTO THE COURTYARD.

→ THE EXTERIOR IS CONSTRUCTED FROM
  REINFORCED CAST-IN-PLACE CONCRETE.

↑ THE INTENSE MEXICO CITY SUNLIGHT PENETRATES DEEP INTO THE LOWER LEVELS OF THE HOME.

→ THE LANDSCAPING IS DESIGNED TO HAVE A WILD QUALITY THAT FEELS ORGANIC AND TIMELESS.

Casa Sierra Fría

Esrawe Studio

MEXICO CITY, MEXICO

At first glance, one would not expect the calm oasis hidden within this project's blank walls. Glimpses of a secret garden draw the visitor into the design, encountering a series of minimal rooms that focus on a sheltered green space. Built in a U-shape, the structure wraps around this courtyard, creating a feeling of introspection and intimacy. Created for a family of four, the central landscaping also anchors the various social and private areas of the home. The architects carefully selected an expressive palette of materials: rugged rust-red brick, used for the exterior walls, contrasts with the smooth wood and stone surfaces found indoors. A roof garden and terrace provide additional outdoor space in a tight footprint. This is the first residence Esrawe Studio has designed, having made a name for itself in furniture and interiors. The studio has achieved a quietly luxurious home, full of calming spaces waiting to be discovered.

↑   THE VIEW OF THE SECLUDED AND VERDANT COURTYARD FROM THE MAIN LIVING AREA OF THE HOME.

↑ GLIMPSES OF GREENERY BEYOND THE TEXTURED BRICK WALLS DRAW YOU DEEPER INTO THE HOME.

← THE LUSH PLANTING OF THE COURTYARD AND ROOF GARDEN FILLS THE CENTER OF THE U-SHAPED DESIGN.

→   A STATEMENT CANTILEVERED STAIRCASE CAN BE SEEN FROM THE CENTRAL COURTYARD, LEADING TO THE UPPER FLOORS.
↓   A WIRE TRELLIS AND HANGING BASKETS ENCOURAGE GREENERY TO GROW UP THE COURTYARD WALLS.

↑   EVEN THE BATHROOM PROVIDES AN OPPORTUNITY TO BRING NATURE INTO EVERYDAY LIFE.

↑ THE FRONT ENTRANCE FEATURES A
   TOWERING WOODEN DOOR, WHICH PIVOTS
   OPEN TO REVEAL THE INNER SANCTUM OF
   THE HOME.

↗ THE MONOLITHIC BRICK WALLS OF THE
   EXTERIOR HAVE NO VISIBLE OPENINGS—
   CULTIVATING MYSTERY AND INTRIGUE.

→ DYNAMIC LAYERS OF PLANTING
   CONTRAST WITH THE MATERIALITY
   OF THE BRICK AND GLASS FACADE.

Index

Evergreen Architecture

Overgrown Buildings and Greener Living

This book was conceived and edited by gestalten.

EDITED by Robert Klanten and Elli Stuhler

INTRODUCTION by Rosie Flanagan
PROJECT TEXTS by Aoi Phillips

EDITORIAL MANAGEMENT by Sam Stevenson

DESIGN, LAYOUT, AND COVER by Capucine Labarthe
HEAD OF DESIGN: Niklas Juli

PHOTO EDITOR: Madeline Dudley-Yates

TYPEFACE: Sprat by Ethan Nakache

COVER IMAGE by Precht
BACKCOVER IMAGES by Lukas Wassmann (top left), Grant Harder (top right),
CHANG Architects (bottom right), Hufton + Crow (bottom middle), and
Koichi Takada Architects (bottom left)

PRINTED BY Gutenberg Beuys Feindruckerei GmbH, Langenhagen
Made in Germany

PUBLISHED by gestalten, Berlin 2021
ISBN 978-3-96704-010-4

2nd printing, 2022